In the Goal

LEVEL 3

/oa/
/ai/

DECODABLES BY jump!

Teaching Tips

Yellow Level 3

This book focuses on the phonemes **/oa/ai/**.

Before Reading

- Discuss the title. Ask readers what they think the book will be about.
- Sound out the words on page 3 together.

Read the Book

- Ask readers to use a finger to follow along with each word as it is read.
- Encourage readers to break down unfamiliar words into units of sound. Then, ask them to string the sounds together to create the words.
- Urge readers to point out when the focused phonics phonemes appear in the text.

After Reading

- Encourage children to reread the book independently or with a friend.
- Ask simple questions about the text to check for understanding. Have them find the pages that have the answers to your questions.

This edition is published by arrangement with Booklife Publishing.

5357 Penn Avenue South
Minneapolis, MN 55419
www.jumplibrary.com

Decodables by Jump! are published by Jump! Library.

Library of Congress Cataloging-in-Publication Data is available at www.loc.gov or upon request from the publisher.

ISBN: 979-8-88996-810-8 (hardcover)
ISBN: 979-8-88996-811-5 (paperback)
ISBN: 979-8-88996-812-2 (ebook)

Photo Credits

Images are courtesy of Shutterstock.com. With thanks to Getty Images, Thinkstock Photo and iStockphoto. Cover – Barcin. 4–5 – PeopleImages.com – Yuri A. 6–11 – PeopleImages.com – Yuri A, Fotokostic, aabejon. 15 – Shutterstock.

Can you find these words in the book?

coach

coat

fail

goal

sail

If they get a lot of goals they can win.

This is Raina in the coat. She is the coach.

Coach tells them to run.

Coach tells them to kick hard.

They run to the net.

She kicks it. Will it go in the net or will it fail?

It will not fail. It will sail into the net.

They win! It was a lot of fun.

Can you say these sounds and draw them with your finger?

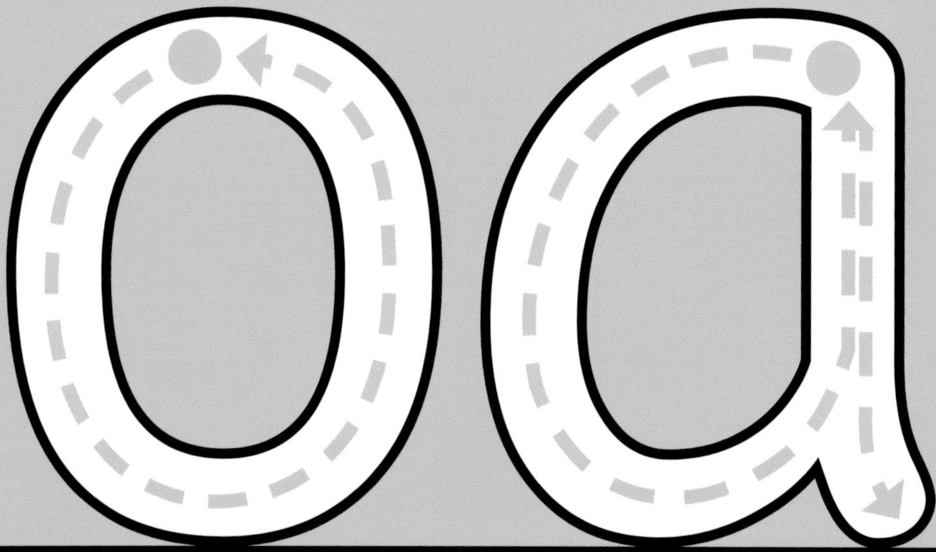

ai

Trace the missing letters to complete each word:

coat

goal

sail

What other words do you know with the sounds /oa/ or /ai/?

soap

boat

snail

mail

Practice reading the book again:

If they get a lot of goals they can win.
This is Raina in the coat. She is the coach.
Coach tells them to run.
Coach tells them to kick hard.
They run to the net.
She kicks it. Will it go in the net or will it fail?
It will not fail. It will sail into the net.
They win! It was a lot of fun.